THE BOOK OF LETTERS

An Adventure
in
Reading, Writing, and Spelling.

THE BOOK OF LETTERS

by
Dr. Michael Thomson
with illustrations by
Bryony Jacklin

LEARNING · DEVELOPMENT · AIDS

LDA

To Mum and Dad with love and thanks.

The Book of Letters
LD900
ISBN 0-905114-73-6
© Text Michael Thomson
© Illustrations Bryony Jacklin
All rights reserved
First published 1989   Reprinted 1990, 1991
LDA, Duke Street, Wisbech, Cambs. PE13 2AE England.
Printed in Great Britain by
Ebenezer Baylis & Son Ltd,
The Trinity Press, Worcester, and London.

INTRODUCTION

You are the star in this adventure story. When you read The Book of Letters you will find a Secret Land and look for the Letter Master. You will choose how to go across rivers, up mountains and along dark paths. You will talk to a Yeti, answer the Hermit's riddles, and beat the parrot, as well as many more things.

You must be careful. If you miss the clues and go the wrong way you may die! Then you will have to start again.

There is a very important piece of paper at the back of the book. Ask someone to photocopy it for you. It is your Equipment List. In the Secret Land you will find things to help you. You must write them down on your Equipment List. Write down the equipment number too so you can find it when you need it. If you do not have the right equipment you will have to go back to find it.

Don't forget to make a note of the story number on the Equipment List if you stop reading the book. Then you will know where to start again.

To begin start at number one. Then you will be told what to do. Sometimes you will have a task to do. Check it with your teacher before you go on.

If you have read Word Quest, you will find that this story tells you what happens before the Wizard!

GOOD LUCK!

1

One day you go for a walk in a wood. You see some hills in the wood. There are also some very big trees. It begins to rain. You did not bring a coat with you. You must get out of the rain. You can:

Go into a big cave that you see in the side of the hill - go to 21.
Go into a woodman's shed that you see - go to 39.
Go under a big tree that is by you - 15.

2

You try to go past him in the boat. The man lets fly with his fishing line. It snags the boat. He pulls you in - 42.

3

You take out the BOOK OF LETTERS (31). This has a code that can help.

Use the BOOK OF LETTERS to decode the YETI'S speech. Write the words down in the space under the numbers.

18 11 5 11   10 12 24 18.   18   11 5   4 8 26 5   24 6 12
21 14 11 19 12 24   11 11 11.   18   6 11 9 12   25 12 12 19
14 12 4 24   25 12 6 18 19 17   25 10   5 10   5 11 24 12 1
18 11 5   4 8 18 12 19 17 14 10.   10 26 13   5 11 10
21 11 1 1.

If you were right the YETI steps back to let you go by. As you go by he smiles that smile again. He gives you a metal disc. You see some writing on it. It is the CAPITAL LETTER DISC. Write it on your Equipment List. You will need it later. It is at 63. When you want to go on you can go into a cave that you see - 23 or go up on a path that winds round the mountain - 52.

You walk on. The trees thin out. You are on a forest path. All about you are letters. They lie on the ground and in trees. Sometimes you see bits of letters. You think that they may be of use to you. Go to 34.

f b d h o r c a g p s

5

At last you come to the top of the mountain. You can see for miles. You look to see if you can see the sea! Just then a thin hand grabs you. It is the HERMIT. He lives at the top of the mountain. He looks at you with a red eye. He is very strong. He will throw you off the mountain unless you can answer his riddles.

Write down your answers to the riddles in the space.

1. What goes up when the rain comes down?

2. What goes round but does not move?

3. Why are a tree and a dog alike?

4. What goes up and never comes down?

5. What keeps with you when the sun shines?

If you want some help go to 13.

If you made mistakes go to 25. If you got them right go to 44.

You try to take your boat over to the island. You are just short. You will have to make some vowels long. Will you use the 'k' rule – 28,   your FULL-STOP KIT – 35,   or try something else – 20?

7

You walk on. The PARROT is very cross. It screeches 'Take no notice, hey?' It flies down and gives you a nasty bite. You think that it might be best to tell it about the BOOK! - 74.

8

You go over to the bit of wood. Check your Equipment List. If you have a spade from the words that you made go to 9. If you do not have a spade you have missed a clue. Go back to get your spade - 34. You must read all the numbers to get you back here again.

9

You dig in the ground by the wood. The wood is a box! The old wooden box has the letter 'k' on it. Just as you go to open the box you hear a roar! You see a huge monster rise out of the swamp. It is the KRAKEN! The KRAKEN looks after the 'k' box. You will have to send him back down into the swamp.

Read out these 'tongue twisters' as fast and as clearly as possible.

1. To 'shush' him

    She sells sea shells on the sea shore, and the sea shells she sells are sea shells I'm sure!

2. To soothe him.

    The five fat thrushes think that four finny fishes float thinly.

The KRAKEN sinks slowly back into the swamp. You open the box. Inside you see a spelling rule for the sound 'k' at the end of words. You will need this later. It is at 29. Make a note of spelling rule 'k' (and the number) on your Equipment List. When you want to go on, go to 51.

The rocky ground is very uneven. There are great holes in the ground. You will have to fill in these holes. To do this go to 56.

You ask the HERMIT if he knows of the LETTER MASTER. The HERMIT says he will tell you what he knows. He says that you must use full stops and capital letters. Do you have the FULL-STOP KIT (12) and the CAPITAL LETTER DISC (63)? You can look at them any time.

Put full stops <u>and</u> capital letters to make good sense.

the hermit was called tom he had lived on mount blend for twenty years now he says that the letter master is called peter he lives at stanlake by the sea a town by the coast

You read what the HERMIT has to say. You will have to go to the sea. You start off down the other side of the mountain. You come to a river that flows down the mountain. Will you go down river – 49 or cross the river – 66?

12

THE FULL-STOP KIT

The FULL-STOP KIT has lots of little dots in it. These are the full-stops. A scroll says 'Use these full-stops at the end of a sentence. A sentence is a set of words that make a sense of their own.' You may look at this kit anytime.

Now go back to the place you were.

Here are some clues.

1. What do you need when you go out in the rain? (not a raincoat)
2. What do you find where two walls meet?
3. What sound does a dog make?
4. What do you get when you light a fire?
5. It gets very long in the evening too!

Now go back to 5.

You go to the man. Just then he lets fly with his fishing line. It snags the boat. The man pulls you in - 42.

You take a look under a big tree. It has a huge trunk. It has a nest in the trunk. It is a nest of consonANTS. They are letter-like insects that are not vowels. They bite! They come from South America.

Pick the consonANTS off you. Put a ring around the letters that are consonants (not vowels).

p e f r a u n t u q t o z a l

Now make 5 words with the consonants and vowels.

....

....

....

You get away from the consonANTS. Just as you go you see an old train Ticket. It is the CONSONANT BLEND Ticket. Write it down on your Equipment List.

Consonant Blend Ticket

You can visit a cave you see in the hill - 21 or go to the woodman's shed - 39.

You walk down the forest path. You see a monkey in a tree. It looks down at you. The trees thin out and you find a swamp in front of you. Over this wet and soggy land you see a mountain. You think that if you climb to the top of the mountain you might see the sea. First you need to cross the swamp!

Fill in the swamp by writing in words that make sense. There may be some clues here.

At the _____ of the mountain there is an _____

man. He _____ long grey _____ tied back from his

face. The old man likes to ask riddles. He is very _____

at riddles. One riddle is _____ something you use to

_____the rain off your head. If you do _____ answer

the man's riddles he gets very _____. Sometimes he

may throw you off the top of the _____.

If you fill in the words you can go to the mountain - 40. Keep trying until you use some words that make sense.

17

If you want to read the RHYMING KIT go to 36. Note the story number so you can get back. Then come back to here. Now read on!

Which word rhymes with the word which has a line under it. Put a ring around the rhyming word.

1. I left my <u>coat</u> in the   house, car, boat.

2. We <u>all</u> played   ball, scrabble, cards.

3. I went <u>back</u> to the   shed, shack, house.

4. I left a <u>rag</u> in the   room, car, bag.

5. The <u>pig</u> is   big, pink, dirty.

6. I have come to <u>look</u> for my   bag, hat, book.

7. Put that <u>fish</u> on a   plate, tray, dish.

8. Please <u>get</u> my   coat, dot, pet.

9. I was <u>fast</u> but still came   first, second, last.

If you matched the rhymes go to 38. If you made any mistakes go to 45.

18

It is a MERMAID. She has long green hair and sits on a rock. She asks if you will help her. If you want to help go to 76. If you do not go to 32.

19

You run as fast as you can. The sound still comes close. You cannot get away! Go to 53.

20

Do you have a MAGIC e scroll? If you do go to 57. If you do not you must go back and get one - 79. Then you must read the numbers to get back.

21

You go into the cave. It is dry and warm. The cave is back a long way into the hill. You look at the cave. You see a slab of rock that looks man-made. You try to move it. It moves! Under the rock is a dip in the ground. You see an old book. It is the BOOK OF LETTERS. If you want to look in the book go to 31. Make a note of this number and the Book of Letters on your Equipment List. You may go and look at the BOOK when you need to.

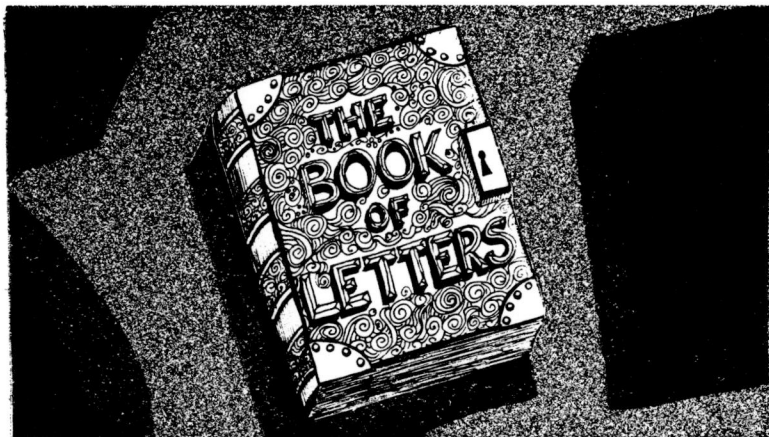

At last the rain stops. You can look in the woodman's shed - 39 or you can look under a big tree - 15.

22

You get on the island. On the island you find a spelling rule. It is the SOFT g rule. Write it down on your Equipment List. When you need it, it is at 75. When you want to go on - 69.

23

You go into the cave. It is very dark. At last you get used to the dark. There is nothing here. It is a dead end - 47.

24

The STATION MASTER lets you have some CONSONANT BLENDS. Did you bring a BAG with you from the useful words (34)? If you did not you will have to go back and get one.

Then you must read the numbers to get back here. (Check your Equipment List.) If you have got a BAG you can put a pile of blends into the BAG. Write down 'CONSONANT BLENDS' on your Equipment List.

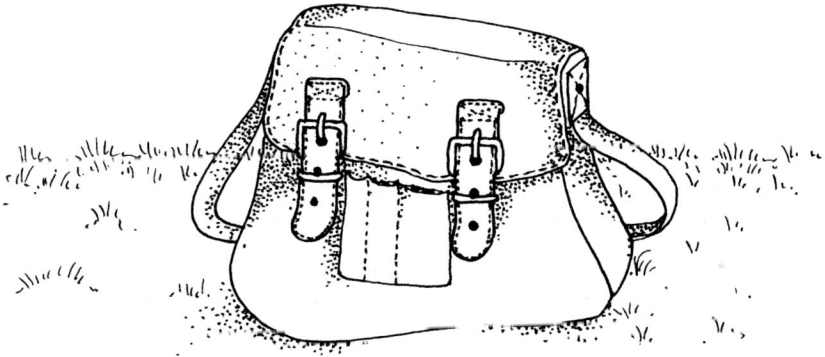

You get back onto the train - 61.

25

The HERMIT throws you off the top of the mountain. Your quest ends!

26

You walk across the open land. Soon more and more trees grow. Then you see a wood path. You go into a wood - 16.

27

The rocks you use are too small. You need to try others. Go back to 56 and use other words.

You pass by the island. Go back to 6.

29

THE k RULE

The sound `k' at the end of words can be -ck or -ke. If the vowel before `k' is short (says its sound) use -ck. If the vowel is long (says its name) use -ke. This is the `magic e'. Here are some words. Read them and you will see how the rule works.

-ck	-ke
tack	take
snack	snake
smock	smoke

Now turn back to where you were. You can come back and read this anytime.

30

You get past the rapids. The boat goes on down the river. After a little time you come to the end of the river. The river meets the sea. At the end of the river you see a very big man.

He must be 8 feet tall. He is fishing. Will you go past him - 2 or stop and ask him the way - 14?

You open the BOOK. You read

'This book comes from the Land of Letters. It has been sent to your world. We hope that if you read this book you can help us. Come to the Land. We have made a path into a shed in your world. Help us!

We have also made a secret code for letters. This may help you in the times ahead of you. In this code each letter has a number. You will need this code later.'

1 = s	7 = q	13 = u	19 = n	25 = b
2 = c	8 = r	14 = l	20 = x	26 = o
3 = k	9 = v	15 = w	21 = p	
4 = f	10 = y	16 = z	22 = g	
5 = m	11 = a	17 = d	23 = j	
6 = h	12 = e	18 = i	24 = t	

So, in this code 'cat' is 2 11 24 and the word 'tin' is 24 18 19.

You can look at this book anytime. Make a note of the number.

Now go back to the place you were.

You go on along the beach. After a while you come to a house. You knock on the door. An old man comes out. It is the LETTER MASTER! You ask him about the problem of the letters. He says that it is all in the Past.

You will have to make the present into past! If you have the LAW OF THE TENSES go to 68.

If you do not you will have to go back and help the MERMAID – 76.

33

You walk on. The shape comes close to the beach. It is a MERMAID. She has long green hair. She asks if you will help her. If you want to help - 76. If you do not want to help - 85.

34

You will try to make some useful words.

Put these 'bits' of words together to make real words. Cross off the bits as you use them. Write the words in the spaces.

ag   b   ade   ch   _____   _____   _____

f   sp   ip   ood   _____   _____   _____

op   fr   t   og   _____   _____   _____

Now write down 3 of these words on your Equipment List. Choose the three you think you will need!

If you need some clues go to 83.

You then hear a sound. It sounds like 'th, ch, wh, sh'. You can walk to the sound - 53 or try to run away - 19.

35

You stop for a while but are not at the island - 6.

THE RHYMING KIT

The RHYMING KIT tells you that some words in English 'rhyme'. That is, they sound alike. Cat and mat rhyme. Pin and win rhyme. Coat and boat rhyme. Cat and cot do not rhyme. You can see that the words that rhyme have endings that have the same letters. Most rhymes are like that. (Sometimes words may rhyme but do not have the same letters at the end. Rough and stuff rhyme.) This RHYMING KIT is for words that rhyme and have the same letters at the end.

The kit has sounds to listen out for. It has letters to look out for. You can look at this kit when you want. Now go back to the place you were.

You head for the rapids. The water goes faster and faster. You see froth and spray. You can see rocks sticking up out of the water. You will have to push the rocks out of the way with real words.

To make real words use the letter consonant rocks b, c, f, l, g, p, r, and s with these letter patterns. One letter has been done. Write the words under each letter pattern.

_old   _ace   _all

bold

If you made a mistake correct it before you are smashed by the rocks. If you got them right go to 30.

The GHOST has gone. You see the GUARD again. He is a very fat man. He is huge! You tell him about the GHOST. He seems to think that you have been dreaming. He asks for your Ticket again! This time he sees that it is a CONSONANT BLEND Ticket. He tells you that this means that you can get some CONSONANT BLENDS from the STATION MASTER at Blend Stop. Just then the train pulls into a station. You can get out here and look around - 77 or go on to the next station - 61.

You go into the shed. Have you got the BOOK OF LETTERS and the CONSONANT BLEND Ticket? If you do not you will need them. You will have to go to the cave - 21 or the tree - 15, to get them.

You see a strange door at the other end of the shed. It has a lock on it. You will have to open it. You can do this by the secret code.

Use the code in the BOOK OF LETTERS to read the words.

26 21 12 19, 1 12 2 8 12 24, 17 26 26 8!

Write down the words here_____

If you were right the door opens. You see a secret land there - 50.

You walk across the swamp. You are at the end of the swamp when you see something in the swamp. It looks like wood. There is a huge tree nearby. If you want to look at the wood go to 8. If you want to go on - 51.

41

At last you come to some rapids. You will have to go over or 'shoot' the rapids to get on. You also see a small island in the river. Will you go over (shoot) the rapids now – 37 or look on the island – 6?

42

The man is the GIANT. He says 'So, what have we here?' You think that he may be fishing for people to eat. You hope not. You ask him the way to the LETTER MASTER. He says that he will help if you can do the 'g' task. You will have to use the SOFT 'g' RULE (see 75). It is the only way you will make the GIANT gentle. Make a note of the number.

SOFT 'g' – Put a ring round the words where the 'g' says 'j'.

glove	guy	gender	gang	gentle
genius	grape	grass	giraffe	gym
gypsy	gent	gasp	gash	germ
gas	gin	guest	green	gyrate
guide	glass	gate	grub	giant

Make two sentences using two of the words you have chosen.

1._____

2._____

If you do not find all the 'j' sounds the GIANT will not be happy. When you are right go to 60.

43

You walk on. The trees thin out. At last you find that you are on an open road. You see letters and bits of letters on the ground. You think that they may be of use to you. Go to 34.

44

The HERMIT is not happy that you got his riddles. Still, he invites you to his shack for a bite to eat. There are old scrolls all over the place. The HERMIT asks if you would like one. You may be able to use it later. If you want to take it - 80. If you do not want to take it - 81.

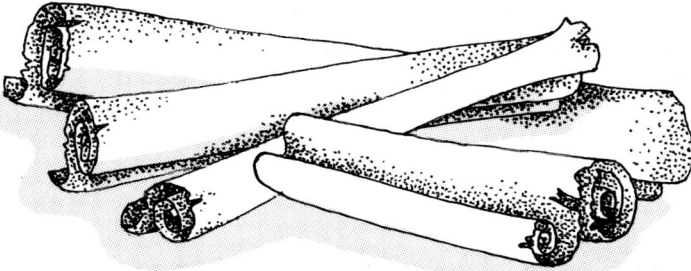

45

Look at the RHYMING KIT again (36). Note this story number first. Now write down a word that rhymes with these words.

wine   _____

boat   _____

sing   _____

flat   _____

If you wrote rhyming words go to 38. If not keep on till you do. Then go to 38.

You will have to go back up the line to 77 to get some.

You have come to a place of End Blends. Here you see letters and sounds at the end of words.

Fill in the end nasal blends -ng or -nk:-

1. I went up the ga . . pla . . into the ship.

2. The ship spra . . a leak and sa . . .

3. Bri . . the washi . . to the si . . .

4. Bri . . the thi . . s with you to the ba . . .

5. I flu . . a rock at it, but it did not hit it.

6. The man had a stro . . dri . . .

7. This thi . . has shru . . . Is it a vest? I thi . . it is.

8. I will cli . . to a pla . . if the ship si . . s.

9. He hu . . the hu . . of ham on the hook.

If you were right you see that there is a path open. You go up the mountain again - 5.

The STATION MASTER says he will ask you some questions before you can have any blends. He will ask you if what he says is true or false.

Put a ring around 'True' or 'False'. The first has been done for you.

1. The GHOST had a green body. (TRUE) FALSE

2. The PARROT had an Aunt called Mabel TRUE FALSE

3. The ConsonANTS came from Africa TRUE FALSE

4. The train GUARD is very thin. TRUE FALSE

5. Rhyming words often have the same
   ending. TRUE FALSE

6. The Train was an electric one TRUE FALSE

TRUE ?

FALSE ?

If you were right with your answers go to 24. If you made a mistake go to 82.

49

You can see no way of going down river. You start to wade. You then think that you need a boat. You will swim to the other bank - 66.

You see the Land of Letters in front of you. There are hills, mountains, rivers and lakes. You can cross over a stream that you see - go to 70 or cross some rocky ground - go to 10.

At last you get out of the swamp. You come to the foot of the mountain. You start to go up. It is steep and hard. After a long time you sit and rest. You hear the 'clump, clump' of footsteps. You look behind you and see a big man-like thing. It is very hairy and nine feet tall! It is the YETI, the mountain ape. It tries to talk to you. Is the grin on its face kind or nasty?! Its words all sound like numbers.

Will you use the 'k' rule - 72, the BOOK OF LETTERS - 3, or the FULL-STOP KIT - 55?

You go up the path. The path seems to fade out in the rocks. You come to a big rock face in front of you. It is a dead end - 47.

The 'th,ch,wh,sh' sound is very loud now. You see some metal tracks on the ground. It is a railway. The sound is an old steam train coming down the track! (Try saying 'th,ch,wh,sh' very fast!) Steam and smoke come out of the funnel. The train begins to slow down. You can flag it down and get on. You will have to make the train stop by stopping the steam. Sort out the 'steam sounds'.

Sort out these words into the right family. Write them
down under the correct letters.

chip	them	church	ship	bath	wish	much
shop	chicken	cloth	moth	dash	shut	chap
chop	lunch	thug	crush	the	shed	that

          sh   th   ch

Now write some of these words into 2 sentences.

1._____

2._____

If you sorted the words – 58. If you made mistakes,
correct them and then go to 58.

54

THE MAGIC e SCROLL

The scroll says
'Vowels can be short (say their sound) like the a in mat. Vowels can also be long (say their name) like the a in mate. The 'magic' or 'silent' e at the end of the word 'mate' makes the vowel long. Here are some more words.

Short vowel	Long vowel
win	wine
hop	hope
cub	cube

All the long vowel words have a magic e. Use this!
Now, back to where you were.

55

You get out your FULL-STOP KIT. The YETI does not like it. He shows his teeth. Try something else, quickly – 51.

56

Make the way safe. Fill in the spaces between the rocks. Put in words to make sentences. Use these words:

fox, put, cup, hid, had, box, cap, cubs

The cat _____ in the _____ .

The man _____ a drink from a _____ .

The boy _____ the _____ on his head.

The _____ had ten _____ .

If you chose the right words go to 67. If you made a mistake go to 27.

57

You can look at the scroll at 54. Note this story number first. Then come back here!

Short and long sounds of the vowels i/o/u. Pick the word to make sense

1. hid   hide

I told my brother to . . . . and he . . . behind the cupboard.

2. kit   kite

My father gave me a . . . to make a big . . . . . .

3. pip   pipe

She got a grape . . . stuck in her wind . . . . . . It made her sick.

4. hop   hope

'I . . . . you win the . . . , skip and jump race', said Dad.

5. slop   slope

Don't . . . . the water out of the bucket when you go

up the . . . .

6. cubs   cubes

I went to see the bear . . . . at the zoo. The keeper
gave all of them two . . . . . of sugar.

7. us   use

The P.E. teacher told . . that we could not . . . the
gym.

8. tub   tube

I dropped a . . . . of toothpaste into the bath . . . .

If you were right – 22. If you made a mistake correct it
and – 22.

58

The train stops and you get on.
You walk along the train.
The GUARD asks for your ticket.
If you have a CONSONANT BLEND
ticket go to 65. If you do not have
a ticket go to 59.

59

You need to get a ticket from the tree in the park.
You will have to go back to the beginning. Go to 1.

The GIANT tells you that the LETTER MASTER is only a short way along the beach. You thank the GIANT and set off along the beach. After a time you hear a cry. You see something in the water. It is calling to you. Will you go to the water and see what it is - 18 or take no notice - 33?

61

You go on down the track to the next station. You get off at the End Stop. If you have some CONSONANT BLENDS go to 62. If you do not you will have to get some. Then you must read the numbers to get back - 46.

62

You can find out more about consonant blends here.

Consonant blends can be at the beginning, middle or at the end of words. Put a line under any of the consonant blends that you can find on this notice.

This is the last stop. From this place you can step onto the steep slopes of Mount Blend. Those of you from the train must go past the stop to get your FULL-STOP KIT. Take care in the swamp which is full of slimy frogs and nasty things.

You need to find more than twenty blends to go on. If you did you can get your FULL-STOP KIT from this station. If you did not, keep trying. Write the FULL-STOP KIT on your Equipment List. You will need it later. It is at 12. You now go on. This is the end of the line so you must walk. You can go into a wood path again - 16 or go across some open land - 26.

It is the CAPITAL LETTER DISC. The words say:
'Use a capital letter at the beginning of a sentence.
Don't forget that a sentence ends in a full-stop. You also
use capital letters for the names of people and places.'
Now go back to where you were. You can read this at
anytime.

64

The MERMAID finds her comb. She is very glad. She
tells you of an old law. It is called the LAW OF THE
TENSES. Write it on your Equipment List. You can look at
it on - 71. You wave good-bye. The MERMAID sits on a
rock. She uses her comb and sings. This is what
mermaids seem to do in a lot of stories! You go on - 32.

You find a seat. The train goes on for miles. It gets
dark outside. You begin to fall asleep. The train clacks
over the track. The rhythm makes you sleepy. In the
dark a shape can be seen. It comes out of the sound of
the wheels. It is the RHYME GHOST. It says

'It seems that once again
There is someone upon my train
You will have to find my rhyme
If you are to get there on time'

The GHOST is a green colour. It sets you a task. You can
use your RHYMING KIT - 17 or read the BOOK of LETTERS - 84.

You try to cross the river. It is too deep. You fall over.
The river takes you down stream very fast. At last you
are going to get to the bank. You are in luck. You find
the HERMIT's boat. You feel that he would not mind you
using it. You set off - 41.

You cross safely. The trees get very tall. The trees are
very close together. You are in a jungle. There may be
some nasty things here. You hear a loud screech.
Something green, red and blue flashes by in the trees.
It is a GIANT PARROT. The PARROT has a very sharp beak.
It asks you where you are going. Will you tell it about
the BOOK? - 74 or walk on - 7?

You can look at the LAW OF THE TENSES if you like (71). Note this story number first.

Put these sentences in the p<u>ast</u> tense

1. I am going to the sea.
2. I see the Yeti near the swamp.
3. I run to get away from the giant.
4. The Hermit tells me to go to the sea.
5. The train stops for me.

When you have made all these into the Past go to 73.

69

You get back on the boat. Now is the time to shoot the rapids! - 37.

70

The stream has rocks across it. They can make stones to step on. You will need to place some more rocks in the stream. To fill in the spaces go to 56.

71

THE LAW OF TENSES

There are three main 'tenses'. Tense is to do with time. There is the Past tense. The Past tense is what went on in the past, like a minute ago, yesterday, last week or last year. The Present tense is what is going on now. Right this minute or today. The Future tense is what will happen, like next minute, tomorrow or next year. Sentences can be written in Past, Present or Future.

Past.	Present.	Future.
I ate a cake.	I am eating a cake.	I will eat a cake.

Now go back to where you were.

72

You look at the 'k' rule (29). This does not help - 51.

73

The LETTER MASTER says that you have done well. He gives you a present. It is a gold BOOK OF LETTERS. The pages are made of gold. The letters are silver, 'This will make you a MASTER OF LETTERS too' he says. The LETTER MASTER then tells you that your time in the LAND OF LETTERS has been a test. You have passed the test! He tells you that an EVIL WIZARD has come into this land. He plans to take all the letters and words of the land. No one will be able to speak or read. A brave person will be needed to stop the wizard. You have shown yourself to be brave so you are the one! Go to 86 if you want to take up the task.

You tell the PARROT about the BOOK. It puts its head to one side and tries to look wise. The PARROT gives you a test. It says 'If you can beat me at saying some sounds I will tell you more!'

Say the sounds of these letters; i, o, m, a, f, t, u, w, s, e. You must say them in less than 8 seconds to beat the PARROT.

If you beat the PARROT go to 78. If you did not keep trying until you are faster than 8 seconds. Then go to 78!

THE SOFT g RULE

This rule says that if there is an e, i or y after the letter 'g' in a word, the g sounds like 'j'. So the word 'gem' sounds like 'jem', the word 'giant' sounds like 'jiant' and the word 'gym' sounds like 'jim'. The words got and gum sound like they are spelt. The g has o after it in got and a u after it in gum.

Now go back to the place you were on.

76

The MERMAID tells you that she has lost her comb. She will have to use a 'k' sound to help her find it. You can help with the 'k' sound at the end of words. Do you have the 'k' spelling rule scroll? If so you can look at it (29).

Put _ke or _ck (sometimes you can use both) after these letters. Write them under the right heading. Two have been done.

ba . .   fa . .   sna . .   sli . .   hi . .   ne .

ro . .   smo . .   mu . .   pu . .   stri . .

_ke   _ck

bake   back

If you were right go to 64. If you made mistakes go back and try again. Then go on.

You get off the train. You are at the Blend Stop. You see a very thin man. It is the STATION MASTER. You show him your CONSONANT BLEND Ticket. He tells you that a consonant blend is two or more consonants that go to make one sound (like cr, pl, str). He shows you a pile of CONSONANT BLENDS. Go to 48.

Blend stop

78

The PARROT is a bit unhappy that you beat its best time. Still, it tells you that there is something going wrong with the letters in the Land of Letters. It tells you that you will need to find LETTER MASTER. It can tell you more. It says that LETTER MASTER lives by the sea. You will have to go and find him. Before you go the PARROT gives you a RHYMING KIT. This helps you with some letter sounds. (Sounds are things that parrots are good at). Make a note of the RHYMING KIT on your Equipment List. It is at 36. Make a note of this number. You will need it later.

The PARROT starts to tell you its life history. It says that it has an Aunt called Mabel. You hurry away!

Now you can try and find the LETTER MASTER. You can go by the forest path - 4 or on the open road - 43.

You think about the scroll the Hermit tried to give you. It may help. You go all the way back to the top of the mountain. You find the MAGIC e scroll by the shack. You will need it later. It is at 54. When you want to go on go to - 11.

You take the scroll. It is the MAGIC e scroll. Write it on your Equipment List. If you want to look at the scroll go to 54. When you want to go on go to 11.

You do not take the scroll. The HERMIT shrugs and throws the scroll out of the shack. Go to 11.

You can find the clues at 78, 65, 38, 15, 53, and 36. When you have read these try again at 48.

You may have to do some digging.

What if you get hungry?

How will you carry all your equipment?

Go back to 34.

The BOOK will not help you, go to 17.

As you walk on her shouts get louder. You go back to help – 18.

86

You can meet and fight the WIZARD in a book called 'Word Quest'. It is like this book. Some of you may even have met the WIZARD in that book. If you have, do not tell any one else his secrets.
If you have not met him – good luck! This is the end of this tale.

THE END

EQUIPMENT LIST

Adventurer, here is your Equipment List. Use it when you write down equipment you find on your journey. Write down its number too.

If you stop reading write down the number you are on. Then you will know where to start next time.

Equipment	Number	Story Number